Cleo the Cold Fish

A Self Help Book for the Child in You

BY MAJO
ILLUSTRATED BY ADRIENNE BROWN

ISBN: 153072516X
ISBN 13:9781530725168

CLEO WAS A COLD FISH.

Although the other fish liked him and enjoyed being around him, Cleo found it difficult to warm up to them. His friends included him in their games and parties, but Cleo was always suspicious of their motives and would ask himself, "I wonder why they like me. They probably feel sorry for me because I'm such a weakling... a name some of the bigger fish still call me. I'll bet if they really knew me they wouldn't like me at all."

BUT THE OTHER FISH DID like Cleo and this baffled him. Sometimes it made him feel even colder towards them. If his team won at flipper ball, he would not join in with all the rubbing and high fin slapping the other fish so enjoyed. It made him feel uncomfortable and uneasy. He chose to busy himself by picking up the balls and other equipment. That way the other fish could not swim too close or nudge him.

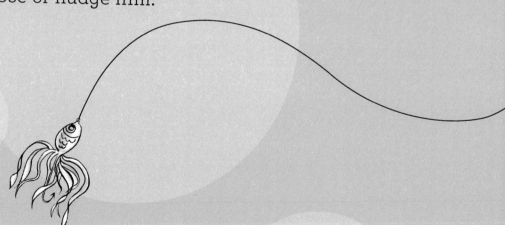

EVEN WITH HIS FAMILY, it was difficult for Cleo to show affection. Cleo loved all his family, but when he tried to express this he felt awkward. The words just stuck in his mouth like some rusty fishhook.

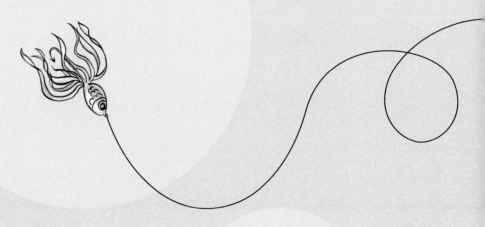

WHILE OTHER FAMILY MEMBERS GREETED each other by slapping tails and swimming happily together, Cleo would give a quick shake of his tail and off he would swim to the back of the lagoon to be by himself. He stayed at a safe distance so that he could hear the other's laughter but not get involved in their frivolity. Cleo pretended such things were silly. He had much more important things to do.

"They know I love them," he thought to himself. "I don't have to tell them."

BUT, JUST TO BE SURE they knew, Cleo would do all sorts of nice things to show his love. He would clean the seaweed off his bedroom floor, take his little sister for a swim, and always share his daily catches with the rest of his family.

9

HOWEVER, CLEO DID LOVE TO listen to his Uncle Morty tell his fisherman stories. Everyone knew Uncle Morty exaggerated when he told about the fishermen he drove crazy. He would pretend to be caught and then, right before they pulled him into their boats, he would jump off the hook. In his trophy case, Uncle Morty claimed to have over twenty-five fishing rods that frustrated anglers had thrown into the water after he got away...but no one had ever seen any of those "rods".

CLEO WISHED HE COULD BE like his Uncle Morty, a happy-go-lucky fish. He wished he could tell his uncle how much he really loved him and how happy he felt when he knew Uncle Morty was coming to visit. But Cleo was afraid his uncle might make fun or joke about Cleo's feelings. "After all," he thought, "Uncle Morty never takes anything seriously."

AND SO, NO MATTER WHO or what the situation, it always seemed to Cleo that he had to keep his distance.

ONE DAY, WHILE CLEO WAS swimming alone, a shimmering, shiny object caught his eye. It seemed to dance in the cool black water like a dazzling silver fish. Cleo had never seen anything so beautiful. He felt curious and decided to swim closer to get a better look at this foreign invader. He poked it with his nose and the silver dancer whirled around and around like the blades from the motor boats. It hit Cleo on his head with a CLUNK. Cleo was stunned and backed away from the mysterious object. Cautiously, he swam closer... but not too close. Cleo caught his reflection in the movement of this silver fish and thought, "This must be a joke. Someone is trying to trick me."

"WHO DO YOU THINK YOU are!" he gurgled as he swam furiously around it. "I'll teach you not to fool with me!"

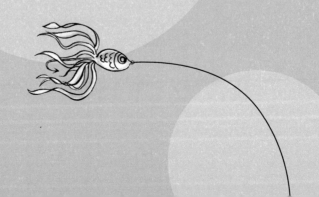

WITH THAT, CLEO OPENED HIS mouth wide to reveal his sharp teeth. He swam furiously toward the dancing object and bit down as hard as he could.

17

UNEXPECTEDLY, CLEO FELT A SHARP pain in his mouth. The feeling was unlike anything he had ever experienced before. Suddenly, he was being pulled powerfully through the currents of the water. The more he resisted, the more the pain stung. It dug into the corners of his opened mouth.

HE WATCHED AS THE DARKENED coolness of his familiar world was whisked away. Violently, he was hoisted out into a bright world that was unfamiliar and frightening.

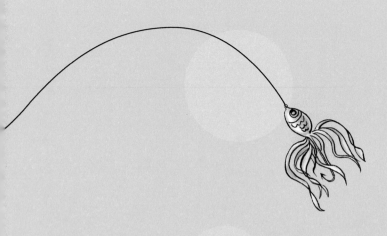

AS HE HUNG DANGLING IN the dry hot air, he could feel his slick skin begin to tighten with the heat.

HIS EYES FELT PARCHED AND sandy.

THE SCALES ON HIS BODY began to itch. He wiggled his frame in an attempt to scratch them. The more he wiggled the more his mouth throbbed.

CLEO HEARD VOICES SHOUTING IN excitement.

"WHAT'D YOU CATCH?"

"IT'S TOO SMALL."

"WHAT KIND IS IT?"

"AH, THROW THE LITTLE THING back."

"KEEP IT. IT'S THE FIRST thing we caught all day."

THE VOICES WERE LOUD AND threatening.

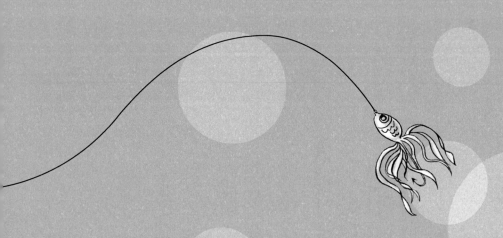

"WHERE AM I?" CLEO WONDERED. "Everything looks so strange. Are they the fishermen Uncle Morty joked about? I wanna go home." He sobbed and sobbed and sobbed.

CLEO WAS STILL NOW. LIMP and exhausted, he just hung there, feeling his heart beat slower and slower.

IN HIS STILLNESS, CLEO THOUGHT he heard another voice. It seemed to be speaking to him from deep down in his gills.

"WELL, CLEO, LOOKS LIKE YOU'RE at the end of your rope, so to speak." The voice did not say this mockingly, but more in a tender, gentle tone… like water swaying against a pier.

"WHAT CAN I DO?" CRIED Cleo. "I think I'm gonna die here… and I'm pretty sure I've never really lived."

"WHY? WHAT HAVE YOU BEEN doing with your life?" the voice asked soothingly.

"NOT MUCH," CLEO ANSWERED. "I guess I've always held back and watched it pass… played it safe… kept my distance. I've never felt free enough to hug and let myself get close."

"I WAS TOO SERIOUS… Maybe tomorrow I'll make some changes is what I always thought."

"WHAT A FOOL I'VE BEEN," Cleo said sadly. "Now I have no tomorrows left."

"LIFE IS MEANT TO BE lived" said the calm voice. "It's a gift, a very precious gift. Life is not meant to be squandered, or taken for granted."

CLEO COULD BARELY BREATHE NOW.

31

"CAN YOU HEAR ME, CLEO?" The voice bellowed.

"YES," HE WHISPERED.

"DO YOU THINK YOU WOULD change if you had another chance?"

"I'D TRY," CLEO REPLIED... EVER so softly.

SUDDENLY, CLEO FELT A TIGHT grip on his limp body. His mouth was stretched wide open. Soon he was flying through the air. In the distance, he heard voices yelling, "He's not big enough. Wait till next year."

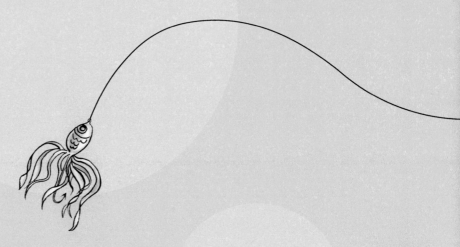

35

WITH A PLOP, CLEO LANDED in the cool refreshing water. Stunned, he just lay there for a few minutes allowing the tide to carry him where it wanted. He wept softly,

GRADUALLY HE FELT HIS GILLS flutter. His tail began to sway.

ALTHOUGH HIS MOUTH WAS ON fire with pain from the saltwater, Cleo didn't notice. He swam home swiftly...shouting... laughing...crying...

"ANOTHER CHANCE... ANOTHER CHANCE...YIPPEE!!!! YIPPEE!!!! ANOTHER CHANCE!!!"

Author Biography

Majo is a wife, mother, grandmother, writer and entrepreneur who promotes positive thinking, and achieving a high quality of life. While raising her family, she began her career as a corporate consultant, training employees in team building, sales and diversity. She also earned a real estate license, wrote a column called "The Family Hour" for a Philadelphia area newspaper, and modeled in print and television. She founded three businesses to foster personal accountability, successful parenting, and improving the prevalent cultural mindset regarding women in advertising.

Of all her many accomplishments, Majo is most proud of being the Mother of her eight children and the grandmother of many. Majo is a beautiful, energetic and determined entrepreneur. She has written six books for children 8 to 80. The first three, *HUMBLE PIE, THE COOL CHAMELEON*, and *CLEO THE COLD FISH*, are now available. *THE DRAB CATTERPILLAR, A DOG AND CAT RELATIONSHIP*, and *LESSONS ON FLYING*, will be available in the near future. It has taken her 30 years and many, many rejection letters to achieve this goal. The saying "It's **never** too late" and Bob Dylan's quote "He who is not busy being born, is busy dying" motivate Majo to keep growing.

Majo is married and lives in Smithville, NJ.

Contact Majo at her website:
majotheauthor.com or email her at mjbgd@aol.com

34014361R00027